OK ETHICS
2014 SPECIAL EDITION

OKLAHOMA
A LEGACY OF VIRTUES AND VALUES

The Oklahoma Business Ethics Consortium is pleased to provide this limited edition copy to select members of the organization who have contributed heartily to the success of the organization over the past ten years and who have robustly promoted Oklahoma values of integrity at work.

Our intention is to celebrate the positive actions taken by prominent Oklahomans, while not always perfect, that have shaped our legacy in a lasting way. We hope that this special book will be a reminder of our heritage and a source of inspiration to all those who read it.

POSITIVE OUTCOMES ARE NOT CREATED BY PEOPLE WHO ARE PERFECT, BUT BY THOSE WHO CONSISTENTLY AND SINCERELY STRIVE TO DO THE RIGHT THING.

2014 Special Edition

OKLAHOMA
A LEGACY OF VIRTUES AND VALUES

Oklahoma Business Ethics Consortium's Special Commemorative Edition

Copyright 2014 by the Oklahoma Business Ethics Consortium.

Published by the Oklahoma Heritage Association

Printed in Canada.

ISBN 978-1-938923-12-8

Library of Congress Catalog Number 2014935685

Compiled by Shannon Warren

Created by Kellian Schneider

Thank You to the Oklahoma Heritage Association for
providing much of the research and numerous photos for this book.

This photo, taken in Tulsa, Indian Territory in 1905, of an early booster club for the chamber who took a band on a rail trip to promote Tulsa. Will Rogers is seated, second from right, in white shirt.

TABLE OF CONTENTS

The Story of OK Ethics

Who Knew? Certainly not the handful of people who started a small discussion group in the fall of 2003. That little group grew by word-of-mouth to nearly double attendance at every meeting for the first few months. The Oklahoma Business Ethics Consortium has grown to **over 1,000 individual members** representing **more than 200 companies**. And, this was primarily accomplished through the efforts of dedicated volunteers.

What started in Oklahoma City as a grassroots effort, kicked into high gear during the summer of 2004, when business leaders and educators from Tulsa and Oklahoma City gathered for a strategic planning session in Stroud, Oklahoma. By then, we figured we were "onto something big" and decided to formalize into what has become known as "OK Ethics." The purpose became clear: to help one another in reinforcing standards of ethical behavior while remaining true to our humble roots.

Now We Know! Most business leaders truly care about integrity in the workplace. In addition to the Consortium's regular monthly forums on ethical issues, OK Ethics annually hosts The OK Ethics Awards. These include the Compass Awards for best practices in business ethics and the Community Impact Awards honoring businesses, non-profits and educational institutions that have uplifted our communities by promoting strong principles, ethical leadership and integrity.

Student Initiatives: At the same time that the Consortium was launched, the OK Ethics Foundation was established to reinforce high standards of integrity among students on various campuses throughout the state. Through OK Ethics' support of local, regional and national ethics competitions, our students have excelled in demonstrating Oklahoma's legacy of honorable behavior and moral courage. For more information about these initiatives, please see page 28 or visit our website at **www.okethics.org**.

Thank You *to these companies for their support of OK Ethics (2013-2014)*

Pinnacle Members

Navigator Members

Star Members & Media Partners

5

Authenticity

"I Never Met a Man I Didn't Like"

Will Rogers

Will Rogers established an enduring legacy that truly captures Oklahoma's spirit. Born in 1879, he was the grandson of a Cherokee chief and son of a senator who helped shape our state's constitution.

Will's first excursion into the public eye involved trick-roping, a skill that he was taught as a youth by a freed slave on his father's cattle ranch in Indian Territory. That talent, along with his endearing wit, opened the door to many opportunities on the world stage. He performed in wild west shows as well as Broadway before graduating to silent films and then "talking pictures." In 1934, he became Hollywood's highest paid actor.

Will's talents didn't stop there. He was a prolific journalist and his homespun wisdom made him a favorite among millions of readers all over the world. A popular political pundit, he was also known as a contemporary philosopher whose gracious outlook inspires us today. Down-to-earth with a heart of gold, he simultaneously embraced his humble roots while befriending others from all walks of life including movie stars, professors and presidents of all political persuasions.

The airport in Oklahoma City is named for Will Rogers, who was killed in a plane crash with Oklahoman Wiley Post in 1935.

Art courtesy of Max Gramling. Source for content courtesy Will Rogers Commission and Memorial Museum, Claremore, Oklahoma. Right picture depicts Will Rogers with other Oklahoma images.

Max Grambling

"A Legacy"

Stewardship

Dr. Harriett Barclay

Ever noticed the roadside wildflower plots? Or, perhaps you've visited the Redbud Valley Nature Preserve near Catoosa? Maybe, you just love to garden?

Then, you will appreciate the work of Dr. Harriett Barclay, a Tulsa botanist and early-day ecologist. Her passion for nature spurred a collection of more than 35,000 plants and 6,000 varieties. In fact, many species have "Barclay" incorporated into their names.

She also initiated the development of Redbud Valley and Oklahoma's first roadside wildflower plots. As we admire the beauty of Oklahoma, we can thank our enthusiastic visionary for much of its preservation.

The Oklahoma Redbud is the state tree of Oklahoma.
Photo courtesy of www.shutterstock.com.

Versatility

Alice Mary Robertson

Long before women had the right to vote, Oklahoman Alice Mary Robertson was appointed America's first female Postmaster by President Theodore Roosevelt in 1905. "Miss Alice," as she was affectionately known, ran the Muskogee post office until 1913. Later, she became the second woman in history to win a U. S. congressional seat.

Quite the Renaissance woman, she began her career as a teacher with the Tullahassee Mission School for the Creek Nation before becoming head of the Minerva Home, a boarding school for girls which was an underpinning for what is now Tulsa University. We applaud her sacrifice through public service and admire this determined woman for her versatility in her life's endeavors.

Innovation

Photo courtesy of the Oklahoma Heritage Association.

Wiley Post

World famous pilot Wiley Post did not always lead a charmed life. In fact, he dropped out of school at age 12, faced personal difficulties and was convicted of robbery. After receiving an early release from prison for depression, he began working as a barnstormer and oil field roughneck. Unfortunately, in 1926, he ran into trouble again when an oilfield accident left him blind in one eye.

Yet, somehow, he prevailed over all of those misfortunes to make many valuable contributions to the field of aviation, including the discovery of the jet stream and invention of the first pressurized flight suit for high altitudes. In 1931, he set a record by making the first solo flight around the world in his famous plane, the *Winnie Mae.*

However, his passion for exploring the skies did not come without a price. He and his good friend, Oklahoman Will Rogers, both met with disaster while flying through Alaska. When this respected Oklahoman's funeral was held in 1935 at the First

Baptist Church in Oklahoma City, more than 75,000 people honored him with their presence.

Wiley Post represents the dogged determination of a fearless Oklahoman who is remembered today for his innovative approach to life and work.

Photos courtesy of the Oklahoma Heritage Association.

THE WINNIE MAE OF OKLAHOMA

LOS ANGELES TO CHICAGO · 9 HRS. 9 MIN. 4 SEC. · AUG. 27. 1930
AROUND THE WORLD · 8 DAYS. 15 HRS. 51 MIN. · JUNE 23 TO JULY 1. 1931
AROUND THE WORLD · 7 DAYS. 18 HRS. 49 MIN. · JULY 15 TO JULY 22. 1933

Photo courtesy of U.S. Air Force photo/Margo Wright.

EARLY YEARS -- WASP Wilda Winfield on photographic mission at Frederick AAF, Frederick, Oklahoma. Photo courtesy of the U.S. Air Force.

Photo courtesy of U.S. Air Force photo/Airman 1st Class Jason Epley.

OKLAHOMANS LOVE TO SOAR!

That could explain why this state has produced so many famous pilots and even a few astronauts, including Thomas Stafford of Weatherford who commanded the Apollo 10 mission in 1969. Colonel William Pogue from Okemah had an amazing career with several NASA missions spanning from 1966 through his final piloting assignment for the Skylab in 1973. He enjoyed soaring so much that, once, he staged a strike to free his crew from the grind of routine drills. They simply wanted an opportunity to reflect on the awe of their celestial experience.

Once a testing ground for Cessna aircrafts and the former home to Braniff Airlines, Oklahoma remains an important aerospace player. According to the Oklahoma Department of Commerce's website, the state boasts an industrial output that exports to 170 countries.

Oklahoma City hosts the central training and support facility for the Federal Aviation Administration (FAA) and the U.S. Department of Transportation. In addition, the Air Logistics Center at Tinker Air Force Base is the largest depot in the U. S. Department of Defense. Many of our OK Ethics members (listed on page 43) are involved in supporting the flourishing aerospace business in Oklahoma.

Photo courtesy of U.S. Air Force photo/Val Gempis.

Celebrating
10 Years!
OK ETHICS
2014 SPECIAL EDITION

Overcoming Adversity

7 Pm May 21 1937 Keyes Okla

Photos courtesy of the Oklahoma Heritage Association.

"Adversity reveals true character. During these storms we lost lives that cannot be replaced. We received scars that will not heal. We also showed others what it is to be an Oklahoman. Faith, family and neighbors. We illustrated what it is to live lives that care about others."

— *Lt. Gov. Todd Lamb in response to Moore tornadoes*

No surprise that Oklahoma is known as "The Heartland." One reason might be because of the way Oklahomans have shown their true heart, even in the face of tragedy. We were tested by the Dust Bowl in the thirties, devastating floods in Tulsa during the eighties, the horrific bombing of the Alfred P. Murrah Federal Building in 1995 and violent tornadoes that have ripped across our state. No matter how dire the circumstances, Oklahomans can be counted on for demonstrating great benevolence, an indomitable determination and undaunted spirit of optimism.

Pictured is the "Survivor Tree" that endured the nearby bombing of the Murrah building, yet continued to flourish. A monument by the elm reads: "The spirit of this city and this nation will not be defeated; our deeply rooted faith sustains us." Courtesy of shutterstock.com.

Oklahoma City National Memorial.

The "Oklahoma Standard"

In 1995, the entire nation staggered in shock when 168 innocent people lost their lives in the horrendous bombing of downtown Oklahoma City's Alfred P. Murrah Federal Building. The world was watching our citizens' reaction to the most vicious act of domestic terrorism that this country had ever seen. That's when the term "The Oklahoma Standard" was born. The actions taken by our people, both then and now, reflect the core of our character. It is best evidenced on the Oklahoma National Memorial & Museum's website, as follows:

"The Oklahoma Standard has been defined as a new level of caring. It was first publicly noted when some members of the media observed that citizens in Oklahoma ran toward the Murrah Building immediately after the bombing, rather than away from the building. When a need for blood was broadcast, it had to be followed by an advisory to stay home, because more people lined up than were needed... First responders from out of town found that they could not go to a restaurant and pay for their own meals... The legend of the Oklahoma Dollar is based upon a first responder commenting that he was leaving Oklahoma with the same dollar he had when he arrived because, during his entire stay in Oklahoma, he had been unable to spend that dollar." — *The Oklahoma City National Memorial & Museum Official Website*

WHAT IS THE OKLAHOMA STANDARD? It is neighbors helping neighbors. It is the spirit of selfless compassion. A resolve to make things better. It is the different faith communities coming together full force with government, medical and other workers to comfort, heal, shelter and protect.

Oklahoma City National Memorial photo courtesy of www.shutterstock.com.

In 2013, after an F5 tornado devastated an elementary school, as well as countless homes and businesses, volunteers rushed to clean up the debris and care for victims. The Oklahoma Standard was once again illuminated in the eyes of the nation.

Photo courtesy of U.S. Air Force photo/Tech. Sgt. Bradley C. Church.

Photo courtesy of U.S. Air Force photo/Staff Sgt. Caroline Hayworth.

Photo courtesy of U.S. Air Force photo/Staff Sgt. Jonathan Snyder.

Generosity

Photos courtesy of the Oklahoma Heritage Association.

Anna Brosius Korn

Time and time again, Oklahomans have volunteered to improve the quality of life for all. They have held fundraisers to support worthy causes and rushed to the aid of their neighbors in trouble. Whether it's running soup kitchens or responding to tragedies like the crushing F5 tornado that hit Moore in 2013, there is a spirit of kindness toward others that is embodied in our state's culture.

That would have made Anna Brosius Korn mighty proud. A woman with vision, Ms. Korn was the driving force behind the initiative to establish what is now known as the Oklahoma Heritage Association. Her intention was to honor people who had provided unselfish service to benefit our great state. This dynamic little redhead devoted countless hours in her efforts to honor Oklahomans who have positively shaped our history. Even well into her 90's, she graciously served her community—epitomizing the caring spirit of volunteerism.

THE SPIRIT OF COMMUNITY

WPX employees helping at Youth Services of Tulsa. Photo courtesy of WPX Energy.

SandRidge Energy employees volunteer to assist the Regional Food Bank. Photo courtesy of SandRidge Energy.

Pictured below is Wadase Zhabwe, a juvenile Bald Eagle whose name means Brave Breakthrough. Her story of resiliency truly reflects the spirit of our great state. She was rescued by the Citizen Potawatomi Nation's Eagle Aviary which is dedicated to the compassionate care and rehabilitation of injured eagles. CPN works diligently to protect these birds, which are considered by them to be "the Creator's great messenger." The Aviary is the first Native American aviary to release an eagle that was banded and fitted with a GPS telemetry backpack harness. They are assisted by volunteers who eagerly track Wadase's return to Oklahoma and report their sightings.

Photo courtesy of Citizen Potawatomi Nation's Eagle Aviary.

Celebrating 10 Years!
OK ETHICS
2014 SPECIAL EDITION

Hospitality

Photo courtesy of the Research Division of the Oklahoma Historical Society.

Ambassador Perle Mesta

Ever wonder where the expression, "the hostess with the mostest" came from? We can attribute it to Oklahoma City's own Perle Mesta. Daughter of hotelier William Skirvin, Ms. Mesta epitomized the spirit of hospitality. Accustomed to hosting lavish parties, she gave a memorable celebration in 1953 when she needed Scotland Yard to guard the jewels of her 125 dinner guests, including the Royal Family.

An enthusiastic political activist, she promoted women's rights through the National Women's Party. Later, she was appointed by President Harry S. Truman as Ambassador to Luxembourg and traveled extensively. She was known in New York, Washington, D.C. and even overseas for her gala parties and fundraising talents. So great was her reputation, that she inspired an Irving Berlin Broadway hit, "Call Me Madam."

"Elegant foods and expensive entertainment aren't prerequisites to a successful party... it's warmth and friendliness that counts."
— Perle Mesta

Visionary

Ella Lamb Classen

Determined to realize her father's dream of settling in Oklahoma Territory, Ella Lamb ventured here in 1890 with less than a dollar in her purse. After working in her uncle's land office, she married a successful entrepreneur: Anton Classen. Together, they built a respected real estate business. After he died in 1910, Mrs. Classen became president—an unusual role for women back then.

She proved to be a generous benefactor to Oklahoma City, donating land for parks and endowing a scholarship fund for graduates of her namesake, Classen High School. Her strong belief in Oklahoma contributed mightily to our state's success.

Photo courtesy of www.shutterstock.com.

Entrepreneurship

Photo courtesy of Rose State College.

Bill Atkinson

Ever wonder how Midwest City got its start? Credit goes to Bill Atkinson, professor, publisher, politician and entrepreneur. Upon learning the War Department might build a new maintenance facility called Midwest Air Depot, now known as Tinker Air Force Base, near Oklahoma City, he quickly bought land adjacent to the area he believed they would choose. His guess turned out to be correct.

In 1942, Atkinson carefully planned what became known in 1951 as an award-wining model city. Later, he helped develop Quail Springs Mall in north Oklahoma City. Today, Rose State College owns his illustrious estate and it is available for tours. We applaud his impressive entrepreneurial spirit in shaping our City.

Humor

Paul Harvey Aurandt

Known as Paul Harvey, this affable radio personality was once responsible for the largest one-man network in the world. Born in Tulsa, his mesmerizing down-home style reached millions of listeners over a span of more than seven decades, including KOMA-AM in Oklahoma City. At one point, he was honored as "the man who contributed most toward the American way of life."

Even today, his famous end note, *"and that is the rest of the story..."* always left us better informed and feeling appreciative of even the simplest blessings in life. Harvey's legacy of good humor and persuasiveness makes us proud that he hails from our great state.

Photos courtesy of the Oklahoma Heritage Association.

2014 SPECIAL EDITION

Determination

Photos courtesy of the Oklahoma Heritage Association.

"I learned from my white students; they learn from me. The beauty of America is in the diversity of her people.
I've never been concerned whether the school officials opposed what I was doing or not.
I was black before I was a schoolteacher, and I'm retiring black."

—Clara Luper

Clara Luper

Clara Luper was not only a history teacher—she was a history "maker."

An award-winning educator, she was known as the mother of the civil rights movement. In 1958, she organized one of the very first publicized sit-ins that our country had ever experienced. Her action prompted an entire chain of 38 drug stores to desegregate their lunch counters not just in Oklahoma, but other states too. A tireless champion of human rights, Ms. Luper also led the initiative to integrate the Oklahoma City Public Schools and was active in Tulsa's first "Freedom Walk" held to promote desegregation of public accommodations.

Ms. Luper led many other freedom initiatives and was arrested 26 times in her pursuit of justice. As a tribute to her efforts, a street near our state capitol now bears her name. It is an honor for an Oklahoma leader who believed in doing the right thing, no matter what the cost.

OK ETHICS
2014 SPECIAL EDITION

Perseverance

Dr. John Hope Franklin

When his mother refused to move to the so-called "Negro" section of a train, a young John Hope Franklin found himself on foot, in the middle of the woods. He overcame the humiliation of racism and rose to greatness, opening doors for many who faced similar difficult circumstances.

Born in 1915 in Rentiesville, Oklahoma and a graduate of Tulsa's Booker T. Washington High School, the Harvard-educated history professor was a key member of the legal team that ended segregation in the nation's public schools. Franklin, a prolific author and respected historian, was the first black professor to hold an endowed chair at Duke University. He epitomized the values of courage and perseverance.

"I want to be out there on the firing line, helping, directing or doing something to try to make this a better world, a better place to live."

—John Hope Franklin

Creativity

Woody Guthrie

Ever been to the Woody Guthrie Folk Festival in Okemah? Their native son wrote nearly 3,000 ballads, including "This Land is Your Land." His work has been performed by everyone from Bruce Springsteen to Bob Dylan. His son, Arlo Guthrie, has followed in his father's footsteps.

In 2013, a museum opened in Tulsa that heralded Woody Guthrie's accomplishments. Surviving the Great Depression and the 1930's Dust Bowl, he was destined to become an iconic American songwriter. Although he was considered a rebel by some who may yet find it difficult to embrace his legacy, he is recognizzed for his spirit of independence and sincere empathy for those who did not have a voice, especially migrant workers.

Photos courtesy of the Oklahoma Heritage Association.

Oklahoma's Future

Rose State College, formerly Oscar Rose Junior College, offered its first classes on September 21, 1970. Since then, it has grown to offer over 60 associate's degree-granting and skilled-occupational programs. It also serves the surrounding community with continuing education courses, festivals, cultural activities and workforce development. Photo courtesy of Rose State College.

The Oklahoma Business Ethics Foundation was started simultaneously with the Consortium's endeavors in 2003. The Foundation's primary mission is to engage students in impactful dialogue that will help them to make prudent, ethical decisions. This is achieved not only by including students in monthly Consortium forums, but also through initiatives undertaken by selfless academic advisors on approximately a dozen campuses across Oklahoma. These include, but are not limited to, the prominent OK Ethics Horizon members who have provided historical photos for this page: Metro Technology Centers, Oklahoma Baptist University, Rose State College and the University of Central Oklahoma.

One of the Foundation's most significant events is the annual Statewide Student Ethics Challenge was started in 2005 on the University of Tulsa Campus and involves undergraduate university students. The day-long event requires weeks of preparation and provides students with an opportunity to crystallize their thinking on dilemmas involving personal integrity, thereby preparing them for ethical challenges that they may face in life. Each fall, winners are coached by a team of prominent business and community leaders during a lively competition. Earmarked funds from dues provided by the Consortium's Pinnacle, Navigator and Star members provide prize money to help winning teams offset costs involved in competing at the Regional Ethics Bowl in San Antonio, Texas and the National Ethics Bowls. For the past two years, participants from the University of Oklahoma and Oklahoma Christian University have achieved success by consistently scoring high in the various contests.

The Metro Technology Centers embrace accountability and ethics as part of their Core Values, finding joy in serving their students through a supportive approach to learning. The main location in Oklahoma City was built on the grounds of the former Springlake Amusement Park. Acquiring the land in 1982, Metro Tech preserved the fond memories of those bygone days by prominently displaying remnants of old rides such as the Big Dipper throughout the campus. Photos courtesy of Metro Technology Centers.

In 1910, Oklahoma Baptist University was incorporated as a higher learning institution in Shawnee and has since grown to include graduate studies in Oklahoma City. Founded on Christian principles, OBU integrates strong moral values with a practical liberal arts education. Pictured above are messengers from the Baptist General Convention of Oklahoma who met on the campus in 1914. Photo courtesy of Oklahoma Baptist University.

The University of Central Oklahoma is the state's largest metropolitan university with more than 17,000 students. Founded in 1890 as a teacher's college, the university embraces "core values of civility, character and community." As an OK Ethics Horizon member, UCO staff and students often attend Consortium meetings. Their scholars have consistently participated in ethics competitions, both locally and nationally. Photo courtesy of the University of Central Oklahoma.

Courage

Anthony Shadid

Anthony Shadid's life was short, but action-packed. Winning two Pulitzer prizes, he was a remarkable journalist covering the Middle East for both the *Washington Post* and *The New York Times*. Even after he was kidnapped in Libya and later shot while investigating a story in the West Bank, the intrepid Anthony Shadid tackled dangerous assignments in areas embroiled in conflict. His reports revealed a depth of understanding as well as compassion for people ensnared by war.

In 2012, at the age of 43, he suffered an asthma attack and died while on assignment in Syria. Even though his career took him far away from his native Oklahoma City, his life's work had an impact far beyond our borders. He continues to serve as an example of extraordinary courage.

2014 Special Edition

Wisdom

Photos courtesy of the Oklahoma Heritage Association.

Thomas P. Gore

Even though he was blind by the age of 12, this remarkable grandfather of famous author Gore Vidal, became one of the first two senators elected after Oklahoma became a state in 1907.

According to the Oklahoma Historical Society's archives, Senator Thomas Gore was a gifted attorney who became a trusted ally of President Woodrow Wilson. He shaped this country by helping to establish the Federal Reserve System and the Federal Trade Commission. As part of the Washington, D.C. scene and highly successful in helping former presidents, he sometimes found himself at odds with those in power. Nevertheless, he did not hesitate to voice concerns, even when the stakes were high.

We salute Senator Gore's remarkable achievements as a man who met challenges head-on and was never afraid to speak truth to power.

Tenacity

Photo courtesy of the Research Division of the Oklahoma Historical Society.

Carl Albert

Standing only 5' 4", Carl Albert may have been short in stature, but he was a powerful force on the national political scene.   Hailing from meager beginnings in a mining shack near McAlester, then later growing up in the tiny town of Bugtussle, the freckled-faced redhead was affectionately dubbed "Little Giant" for his feisty character.

Albert proved to be a brilliant scholar, working his way through the University of Oklahoma on his considerable talent as an orator and sometimes as a driver for Thomas Gore. After graduation, he received a Rhodes Scholarship and studied abroad at Oxford.

In 1946, Carl Albert's campaign for a Congressional seat propelled forward with a slogan that denoted his humble roots: "From a Cabin in the Cotton to Congress." His career progressed and he was elected Speaker of the House in 1971. As such, he nearly became President of the United States twice, following resignations from both Spiro Agnew and Richard Nixon.

As Speaker during the Watergate scandal, Albert tenaciously resisted pressure from those with ambitious agendas who wanted to impede the appointment of Gerald Ford to the Presidency after Richard Nixon's resignation.   As a result of his forbearance, he earned a reputation for being unwaveringly fair.

He retired to his home town in McAlester in 1977, but Albert left an indelible legacy during his lengthy tenure in public office. These include agricultural initiatives, support of the civil rights movement and reformation of legislative procedures that led to greater transparency for the public good.

Resourcefulness

Allen Wright

Ever wonder who came up with the name "Oklahoma"?

Most folks who were born and raised here know that it means "red people," but whose idea was it? While the history of the name has been debated, the credit for the initial suggestion may well be due to a Presbyterian minister and Choctaw statesman.

Named Kiliahote, this bright young man arrived in McCurtain County from Mississippi in 1826. Initially raised by parents who were unaccustomed to speaking English, he was orphaned at an early age and later took the name Allen Wright. Despite early challenges with the language barriers, he became fascinated with learning. He set about getting a solid education and was the first Native American student from Indian Territory, as eastern Oklahoma was known then, to graduate with a Masters of Arts degree from New York City's Union Theological Seminary.   He continued to excel in academic pursuits, preaching as well as ranching, but became the Choctaw Nation's first elected treasurer in 1859. From there, his political career continued to accelerate. When U. S. Commissioners needed a name for consolidation of tribal interests, they liked the idea given to them by the Principal Chief of the Choctaws—Allen Wright.

A resourceful individual, Wright was also known for his superior communication skills. Not only was he relied upon to negotiate treaties, but he also managed to translate the Psalms from Hebrew into Choctaw and created a dictionary for the Choctaw language.

CHIEF WOLF ROBE
WAS A CHEYENNE
LEADER WHO WAS
FORCED TO RELOCATE
TO INDIAN TERRITORY
FROM COLORADO
IN 1877. HE WAS
RUMORED TO BE
THE MODEL FOR THE
NICKEL MINTED IN
THE EARLY 1900'S.

Statesmanship

Governor Dewey Bartlett

Did you know that the term "OKIE," commonly used to describe residents of our great state, is actually an acronym for "Oklahoma: Key to Intelligence and Enterprise"?

The imaginative revival of the term "OKIE" was due to former Governor Dewey Bartlett, who came to Oklahoma to work the oilfields during his college days and stayed, living his life in Tulsa. He was Oklahoma's first governor eligible for a second term in office. A natural leader, he not only enjoyed political life, but the former Marine captain was a successful entrepreneur and rancher.

Photo courtesy of the Research Division of the Oklahoma Historical Society.

Strength

Ambassador Jeane Kirkpatrick

Oklahoma has had many women in leadership, but probably none as colorful as Jeane Kirkpatrick who shaped U.S. diplomatic relations in the early eighties. President Ronald Reagan appointed this conservative Duncan Democrat to serve as our nation's first female United Nations Ambassador. A tough minded leader, she told *The New York Times* in a 1996 interview, *"Power is based not merely on guns or money, but on the strength of personal conviction."* We respect Ms. Kirkpatrick for having the courage of her convictions.

The Oklahoma State Capitol and statue "As Long as the Waters Flow" by artist Allan C. Houser. Photo courtesy of www.shutterstock.com.

Leadership

Photos on this page courtesy of the Oklahoma Heritage Association.

Wilma Mankiller

Wilma Mankiller did not have an easy life.

Born in 1945 at the Indian Hospital in Tahlequah, her family was relocated to California as part of the Bureau of Indian Affairs' (BIA) Relocation Program. Later, she was severely injured in a car wreck and told that she would never walk again. After recovering from the accident, she was then struck by a terrible neuromuscular disease. Despite all these challenges, in 1985 the strong but gentle Mankiller became the first female principal chief of the Cherokee Nation and was later honored with the Presidential Medal of Freedom.

Today, we honor Ms. Mankiller for her perseverance and leadership.

Valor

Admiral Joseph "Jocko" Clark

Who would have guessed that land-locked Oklahoma would produce one of our country's greatest naval officers?

Back in 1893, when Oklahoma was still divided into two territories, Admiral Joseph "Jocko" Clark was born in the area now recognized as Pryor. He became the first Native American graduate of the U. S. Naval Academy and rose to fame as one of the most renowned admirals of World War II. In fact, he was often referred to as the "Patton of the Pacific." During the Korean War, he was an astute fleet commander and introduced close air support measures that became known as "Cherokee strikes."

The highly decorated Admiral Clark reflects the long legacy that Oklahoma has demonstrated in support of the military, including other brave leaders such as Admiral William J. Crowe from Oklahoma City and General Tommy Franks from Wynnewood.

Photo courtesy of U.S. Air Force photo/Master Sgt. Brian M. Boisvert.

Heroic

Photo courtesy of www.shutterstock.com.

Irvin "Bert" Woodring

Did you know that Enid's airport is named after an early day dare-devil? Irvin "Bert" Woodring was a member of the Army Air Corps' early precision flying team known as the Three Musketeers. Born in Enid in 1902, Woodring's flight escapades were legendary and together with another bold Oklahoma pilot, William Cornelius, traveled to new heights in the clouds. Accepting dangerous missions, he received many awards.

Woodring was killed while testing an experimental plane in Ohio in 1933, thus ending his career of passionate dedication to the advancement of aeronautics. However, you might recognize those who have followed the tradition of his fantastic aerial feats, such as those made today by the U. S. Air Force's Thunderbirds.

Stalwart

Photos courtesy of the U.S. Air Force.

Major General Clarence L. Tinker

Tinker Air Force Base in Oklahoma City is named in honor of one of Oklahoma's bravest ancestors—Clarence L. Tinker. The first Native American to be promoted to the rank of Major General, Tinker was born in the former Osage Nation of Indian Territory in 1887. His strategies are credited for playing a key role in protecting the United States, Panama Canal and the Caribbean from further aggression by Japanese forces during World War II. A courageous leader, he boldly engaged in the fierce Battle of Midway in 1942. His plane was lost, making him the first general to sacrifice his life in that war.

Photo courtesy of U.S. Air Force photo/Margo Wright

Growth

Abner E. Norman

Did you know that the name of an Oklahoma town was started by a taunt from survey crews for their supervisor? According to the City of Norman archives, a young Abner E. Norman was contracted in 1870 to survey much of Oklahoma Territory.

Apparently, his crew attempted to ridicule him by burning the words "Norman's Camp" into a nearby tree. The name stuck and now Abner's camp is home to the University of Oklahoma and is the third largest city in the state.

Photo courtesy of the Research Division of the Oklahoma Historical Society.

Compassion

Kate Barnard

Just five feet tall, Kate Barnard was a mighty voice within a tiny frame. This amazing woman had a special place in her heart for the oppressed. Beginning her career as a teacher shortly after the Oklahoma Land Run, Ms. Barnard was deeply moved by the plight of those caught in poverty. She became a passionate activist, rallying women to form powerful alliances to address social injustices. In 1907, she became the first woman to be elected to a major office in Oklahoma. Even though this was well before women had the right to vote, she handily garnered more votes than any other candidates. Today, the Oklahoma Commission on the Status of Women honors her work through an award in her name. It is given to women who, as public servants, have made an extraordinary difference in this state.

"Barnard's efforts led to passage of thirty laws, resulting in child labor reform, compulsory school attendance, a juvenile court and reformatory system for young offenders, orphanages, institutions for the mentally and physically disabled, prison reform, and modern, humane correctional facilities. She improved labor conditions for Oklahomans and brought national attention to orphaned Indian children defrauded of mineral and property rights by court-appointed guardians. Her work paved the way for Oklahoma women's participation in social reform." — Jim Logan, *Oklahoma Today*

Photo courtesy of the Research Division of the Oklahoma Historical Society.

OK ETHICS GUIDING PRINCIPLES

I. Responsibility to Self and Others:

Service:
- Passion for promoting ethics and integrity.
- Encouraging the promotion of ethical behavior through personal actions and sharing ideas and resources.
- Responsibility and accountability for fulfilling the mission of the Consortium.

Collaboration:
- Achievement of common goals through the promotion of ethical, mutually beneficial relationships.
- Service to the Consortium over promotion of self-interest.
- Cooperation emphasized over competition in promoting ethical business conduct.
- Members collaborate by being constructively engaged in discussions regarding ethics.
- Seeking consensus in interactive discussions regarding ethical matters.

Respect:
- Members may become aware of confidential information shared by others in an effort to determine an ethical course of action. We ask members to be sensitive in recognizing and respecting the efforts made toward achieving ethical behavior. In that vein, public disclosure of this information is discouraged.
- We respect other members and the process by:
  - Exhibiting listening skills and actively listening to discussions.
  - Being open to other points of view and outcomes.
- We are an inclusive organization and demonstrate this by welcoming members who are in different stages of learning as applied to ethical behavior.

II. Lead with Integrity

Dependability:
- Members are asked to demonstrate their support of this initiative by consistently attending meetings.

Initiative:
- Recruiting other members who have demonstrated a desire to promote ethical behavior in their organizations.
- Recognizing what needs to be done to help promote the Mission of the Consortium and taking action to assist in that effort.

Honor:
- Members are asked to honor the Consortium through the practice of integrity and ethical behavior in their business dealings.
- We express gratefulness to our hosts, sponsors and speakers.
- Realizing that each of us is in a mode of continual learning, we demonstrate humility, care and compassion when sharing our thoughts and knowledge.

Courage:
- Speak the truth with confidence and encourage others to do the same.

III. Inspire Trust

- We serve and promote the cause of truth with integrity, objectivity and fairness to all persons.
- We hold ourselves accountable by consistently honoring our word.
- We extend trust abundantly to those who have earned it.
- Trust, once earned, will not be taken for granted, manipulated or abused.

HORIZON MEMBERS

American Fidelity Assurance Company
BVA
Chaparral Energy
Cherokee Nation Businesses
Google Inc.
HighMount Exploration & Production LLC
HoganTaylor LLP
Hyde & Company CPAs
Ideal Homes of Norman, LP
Laredo Petroleum
Metro Technology Centers
Nextep
OBU College of Graduate & Professional Studies
Oklahoma Dept. of Commerce
PricewaterhouseCoopers LLP
Rose State College
Rowland Group
TriStar Pension Consulting
University of Central Oklahoma - College of Business

LEADING MEMBERS

Access Midstream
Arvest Bank
Bank 2
BancFirst
Bank of Oklahoma
BKD, LLP
Boeing
Brainerd Chemical
Cole & Reed
Crowe & Dunlevy
Curzon, Cumbey & Kunkel, PLLC (CCK)
Darby Equipment Company
Doerner, Saunders, Daniel & Anderson LLP
Explorer Pipeline Company
Finley & Cook PLLC
First Fidelity Bank
GableGotwals
General Tommy Franks Leadership Inst. & Museum
Leader Communications, Inc.
Learning Unlimited

Legend Senior Living
Luxa Enterprises, LLC
LynnCo Supply Chain Solutions
Mazzio's LLC
McAfee & Taft
OGE Energy Corp.
Oklahoma Sports & Orthopedics Institute
Oklahoma Teachers Retirement System
Parker + Lynch (formerly Accounting Principals)
Principal Technologies
Prosperity Bank (formerly Coppermark)
Public Strategies
Retirement Investment Advisors
Samson Resources Company
Sandler Training
Senior Star
Smith & Kernke
Stinnett & Associates, LLC
Tulsa Technology Center
University of Tulsa
Video Gaming Technologies

TRAILBLAZER MEMBERS

Accel Financial Staffing
AcctKnlowledge
Alliance Resource Partners
American Bank & Trust Co.
Capitol Abstract & Title Co.
Coherent Contracts, LLC
Cornerstone Recruiting Group LLC
4ward Strategy
The Crosby Group
D.R. Payne & Associates, Inc.
Eide Bailly, LLP
First National Bank and Trust Co.
Full Force Marketing & Branding
Gabbard & Company
Mustang Fuel
Oklahoma Allergy & Asthma Clinic
Oklahoma Foundation for Medical Quality
OCU - Meinders School of Business
Oral Roberts University
Red Rock Insurance Company
RL Hudson & Company

Resources Global
Walker Companies
Warren Consulting
Wildcat Well Logging

*OK Ethics has provided free Frontier memberships to certain 501c3, non-government entities.

FRONTIER MEMBERS

1-180 Squadron, OK Army National Guard*
AAR Aircraft Services-Oklahoma
Alzheimer's Association*
Ben E Keith Foods
Better Business Bureau Serving Central Oklahoma*
Black Liberated Arts Center Inc (BLAC)*
CAP (Community Action Project) Tulsa*
Cameron University
Central Oklahoma Humane Society*
Circle of Care*
Delaware Resource Group
Dialogue Institute Oklahoma City*
Dove Science Academy*
Duncan Oil Properties (Walter Duncan, Inc)
Epworth Villa*
The F&M Bank & Trust Company
FATE*
Family Builders*
Feed the Children*

First Christian Church*
Francis Tuttle Technology Center
Girl Scouts of Eastern Oklahoma*
Grant Thornton LLP
Gray, Blodgett & Company, PLLC
Greater Oklahoma City Chamber
Greater Oklahoma City Hispanic Chamber of Commerce
INTEGRIS Health*
Langston University
Masonic Charity Foundation of Oklahoma*
MidFirst Bank
MTM Recognition
National Hispanic Disaster Relief Network*
NewView Oklahoma, Inc.*
OKC Chp of the Institute of Management Accountants*
Oklahoma Association of Realtors*
Oklahoma Center for Nonprofits*
Oklahoma Christian University
Oklahoma Heritage Association*

Oklahoma Society of Land Surveyors*
Oklahoma Quality Foundation*
PMI Oklahoma City Chapter*
REI Oklahoma*
Refuge Fellowship Church*
SALLT and Light Leadership Training Inc.*
SNU - Southern Nazarene University
Single Parent Network*
South OKC Chamber of Oklahoma
Strata Leadership (formerly Character First)
Sunbeam Family Services, Inc. *
The Journal Record
Tulsa Area United Way*
Tulsa Ballet Theatre, Inc.*
Institute of Management Accountants*
Tulsa Global Alliance
United Petroleum Transports
University of Oklahoma, College of Arts & Sciences
Variety Care*

Tony Blasier* James Branscum~ Carla Brockman~ John Burnett^ Deborah Burroughs
Bob Byrne* Tommy Campbell David Carmichael^ Rick Christiansen^ David Christie Lucius
Crandall Barbara Crandall Janice Dobbs*^ Rod Edwards Steve Ellis Lynn Flinn*^ Pam
Fountain* John Foust~ Valerie Fried*^ Garyl Geist* Alicia Goodloe Jamie Gorman
Wayne Hart Jenny Hatton Shannon Hiebert*^ Valorie Hodges Mary Kay Huggard Nancy
Hyde Oscar Jackson~ Travis Jones* James Kelley Joy LaBar* Jan Laub Thomas
Legan~ Neal Lehman Todd Lisle* Tracy Manley Brent Martens Rob Martinek* David
Mayfield* Tammy McKeever Shirley Mears Nick Minden Lynda Mobley* Michael Mount
Karie Mullins Larry Musslewhite^ Sandra Nettleton Mark Neumeister Michael Oonk Doyle
Paden Jacob Pasby Susan Pate Jalisha Petties Marvinette Ponder Jamie Potter Trish
Potter Jim Priest^ Bobby Redinger Ben Robinson Bertha Robinson Steve Rockwell
Connie Root Anna Rosenthal Myrna Schack Latham*^ Kellian Schneider* Colin Schoonover*
Tony A. Scott Jeffrey Simmons John Stancavage Edith Steele~ Howard Stein^ Linda Streun
Mike Strong~ Katherene Terrell Randy Thurman* Bill Turner Mary Vaughn Joe Walker
Shannon Warren*^ Brandy Weldon Susie Wellendorf* Daniel Yunker Tony Blasier*
James Branscum~ Carla Brockman~ John Burnett^ Deborah Burroughs Bob Byrne*
Tommy Campbell David Carmichael^ Rick Christiansen^ David Christie Lucius Crandall

Oklahoma leaders dedicated to promoting integrity in the workplace.

2013-2014

OK ETHICS EXISTS BECAUSE OF THE ONGOING DEDICATION TO OKLAHOMA VALUES OF INTEGRITY AT WORK.

Those listed on this page include academic, business and community leaders, professionals and volunteers who were actively involved in OK Ethics as of March 9, 2014. It is our desire to express appreciation to all those whose names are listed on these pages. They, along with many other individuals, have contributed significantly to the success of OK Ethics mission through various endeavors, from assisting with the Consortium's monthly events or our annual award programs to the Foundation's student ethics initiatives. We are deeply grateful.

* OK Ethics Board Member
^ Founding Member
~ Compass Awards Selection Team

bara Crandall   Janice Dobbs*^   Rod Edwards   Steve Ellis   Lynn Flinn*^   Pam

ntain*   John Foust~   Valerie Fried*^   Garyl Geist*   Alicia Goodloe   Jamie

man   Wayne Hart   Jenny Hatton   Shannon Hiebert*^   Valorie Hodges   Mary

Huggard   Nancy Hyde   Oscar Jackson~   Travis Jones*   James Kelley   Joy

ar*   Jan Laub   Thomas Legan~   Neal Lehman   Todd Lisle*   Tracy Manley

nt Martens   Rob Martinek*   David Mayfield*   Tammy McKeever   Shirley Mears

k Minden   Lynda Mobley*   Michael Mount   Karie Mullins   Larry Musslewhite^

dra Nettleton   Mark Neumeister   Michael Oonk   Doyle Paden   Jacob Pasby

an Pate   Jalisha Petties   Marvinette Ponder   Jamie Potter   Trish Potter   Jim

st^   Bobby Redinger   Ben Robinson   Bertha Robinson   Steve Rockwell

nie Root   Anna Rosenthal   Myrna Schack Latham*^   Kellian Schneider*   Colin

oonover*   Tony A. Scott   Jeffrey Simmons   John Stancavage   Edith Steele~

ard Stein^   Linda Streun   Mike Strong~   Katherene Terrell   Randy Thurman*

Turner   Mary Vaughn   Joe Walker   Shannon Warren*^   Brandy Weldon   Susie

lendorf*   Daniel Yunker   Tony Blasier*   James Branscum~   Carla Brockman~

Burnett^   Deborah Burroughs   Bob Byrne*   Tommy Campbell   David

michael^   Rick Christiansen^   David Christie   Lucius Crandall   Barbara Crandall

ce Dobbs*^   Rod Edwards   Steve Ellis   Lynn Flinn*^   Pam Fountain*   John

st~   Valerie Fried*^   Garyl Geist*   Alicia Goodloe   Jamie Gorman   Wayne Hart

y Hatton   Shannon Hiebert*^   Valorie Hodges   Mary Kay Huggard   Nancy Hyde

ar Jackson~   Travis Jones*   James Kelley   Joy LaBar*   Jan Laub   Thomas

an~   Neal Lehman   Todd Lisle*   Tracy Manley   Brent Martens   Rob Martinek*

id Mayfield*   Tammy McKeever   Shirley Mears   Nick Minden   Lynda Mobley*

hael Mount   Karie Mullins   Larry Musslewhite^   Sandra Nettleton   Mark

meister   Michael Oonk   Doyle Paden   Jacob Pasby   Susan Pate   Jalisha Petties

vinette Ponder   Jamie Potter   Trish Potter   Jim Priest^   Bobby Redinger   Ben

inson   Bertha Robinson   Steve Rockwell   Connie Root   Anna Rosenthal   Myrna

ck Latham*^   Kellian Schneider*   Colin Schoonover*   Tony A. Scott   Jeffrey

ons   John Stancavage   Edith Steele~   Howard Stein^   Linda Streun   Mike

ng~   Katherene Terrell   Randy Thurman*   Bill Turner   Mary Vaughn   Joe

A Few Former OK Ethics Speakers

Devon: Larry Nichols & John Richels

Kimray: Tom Hill

The Williams Companies: Robyn Ewing

ONEOK: John Gibson

Giant Partners: David Woods

Hobby Lobby: Peter Dobelbower

Strata Leadership: Dr. Nathan Mellor

The Journal Record: Mary Mélon & Ted Streuli

Boeing: James Bell (CFO)

KFOR: Kevin Ogle

Jim Priest, Attorney

OKC Police Chief Bill Citty

Sheriff John Whetsel

OKC District Attorney David Prater

Salt & Light Leadership Team: Wes Lane

University of Oklahoma: Joe Castiglione and Coach Sherri Coale

Oklahoma State University: Burns Hargis

Oklahoma City University: Tom McDaniel and Dr. Vince Orza

University of Central Oklahoma: Dr. Don Betz

Oral Roberts University: Dr. Mark Rutland

General Tommy Franks

Former Lieutenant Governors Jari Askins and Mary Fallin

Attorney Generals Mike Turpen, Larry Derryberry, and Susan Loving

General Rita Aragon Secretary of Veterans' Affairs

Former Tulsa Mayor Kathy Taylor

Former OKC Mayor Kirk Humphreys

OKC Mayor Mick Cornett

Covey Link & Smart Trust: Stephen M. R. Covey

Chuck Colson

The Ethics Coach: Gael O'Brien

The Ethics Guy: Dr. Bruce Weinstein

Fish! Author Harry Paul

Author Jim Stovall

OKC Thunder: Sam Presti and Pete Winemiller

Former Governor George Nigh

Joel Manby, CEO & Undercover Boss

Former President of Reebok Dr. Marilyn Tam

Faith leaders: Dr. Bob Long, Father Rick Stansberry & Imam Imad Enchassi

Building Community Institute: Clifton Taulbert

Oklahoma Center for Non-Profits: Marnie Taylor

KTUL Channel 8: Kristin Dickerson

Tulsa World: John Stancavage

World Series Champion, Ed Hearn

Worldcom Controller, David Myers

Pinnacle Members 2013-2014

Bama Companies

PEOPLE HELPING PEOPLE BE SUCCESSFUL

Chesapeake
ENERGY

devon

Since the 1960s, the Bama Companies, Inc. has been an innovator of wholesome bakery products that cater to the needs of the biggest restaurant chains worldwide. Today, the company serves customers in more than 20 countries. They achieve this through vision, leadership, integrity, strategic focus and a single mission of "People Helping People Be Successful." The Bama Companies were honored for high ethical standards when they received the 2007 OK Ethics Compass Award for the large business sector.

Chesapeake Energy Corporation, a founding Pinnacle member, sets high ethical standards for the conduct of its employees and business partners while maintaining an unwavering commitment to finding and producing America's oil and natural gas resources in the most environmentally responsible manner. A leading independent exploration and production company and a top Oklahoma employer, Chesapeake implements programs that promote the health and safety of its employees, partners and the environment and gives back to communities. In 2009 Chesapeake received the OK Ethics Compass Award for the large company category.

Photography by David McNeese courtesy of Chesapeake Energy Corporation.

Devon Energy was one of the fir companies to fully support OK Ethics an was among our first Pinnacle member It is, one of the world's leading independent o and gas producers. The company builds valu for shareholders by creating an atmosphere optimism, teamwork, creativity, resourcefulnes and by dealing with everyone in an honest an ethical manner. In 2011, Devon earned the covete Compass Award for large business and, Lar Nichols, their Executive Chairman, received th Executive Pilot Award for his principled leadershi in shaping his company as well as our great state

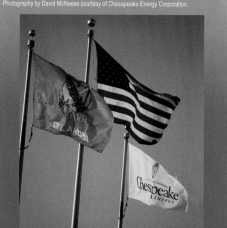

Promoting Integrity at Work in Oklahoma

Kimray is an industry-leading global manufacturer celebrating 65 years of excellence. The company manufactures a comprehensive line of control equipment for the oil and gas industry and is the third largest family-owned company in the state. In 2010, Kimray received the Compass Award and at the same time, Kimray's Chairman, Tom Hill, was honored with the very first Pilot Award for his outstanding commitment to promoting Oklahoma values of integrity at work. As a company, Kimray's vision is "to make a difference in the lives of those we serve: our employees, our customers, and our community."

SandRidge Energy, Inc. is an active participant in the transformation of downtown Oklahoma City. SandRidge also participates in the transformation of lives through both financial investment and employee engagement. Ethics and moral obligation drive the company's mission to make a tangible difference in the communities where their employees work and live.

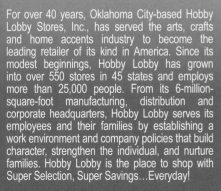

For over 40 years, Oklahoma City-based Hobby Lobby Stores, Inc., has served the arts, crafts and home accents industry to become the leading retailer of its kind in America. Since its modest beginnings, Hobby Lobby has grown into over 550 stores in 45 states and employs more than 25,000 people. From its 6-million-square-foot manufacturing, distribution and corporate headquarters, Hobby Lobby serves its employees and their families by establishing a work environment and company policies that build character, strengthen the individual, and nurture families. Hobby Lobby is the place to shop with Super Selection, Super Savings…Everyday!

Early Glenpool Oil Field. Photo courtesy of the Tulsa Regional Chamber.

BIBLIOGRAPHY

BOOKS & MAGAZINES
Chronicles of Oklahoma, The Encyclopedia of Oklahoma History and Culture
Oklahoma Today Magazine

MUSEUM COLLECTIONS
Oklahoma City National Memorial & Museum
Oklahoma Heritage Association, Hall of Fame Archives
Oklahoma Historical Society, Research Division
Will Rogers Commission and Memorial Museum

NEWSPAPERS
Charlotte Observer
Edmond Sun, The
Los Angeles Times
New York Times, The
Osage News
Washington Post

WEBSITES & BLOGS
www.airforce.com
www.ancestry.com
www.anthonyshadid.com
www.biography.com
www.centennialofflight.net
www.choctawnation.com
www.ci.norman.ok.us
www.dougdawg.blogspot.com
www.history.house.gov
www.history.navy.mil
www.jhfcenter.org
www.newsok.com
www.ok.gov
www.okc.gov
www.oldairfield.com
www.pulitzer.org
www.reuters.com
www.tinker.af.mil
www.willrogers.com
www.woodyguthrie.org

OTHER
Oklahoma Department of Commerce

ACKNOWLEDGMENTS

OK Ethics is deeply grateful for the wonderful submissions made in response to our request for images that captured the spirit of Oklahoma. Unfortunately, we could not use all that were donated, but we were inspired by the efforts made.

We wish to acknowledge those individuals whose pictures were selected for the book as well as thank people who went to extraordinary lengths to support this initiative by sharing their gifts of time and insights. These include: **Artist Max Gramling**; **Beth Dean** and Nextep, Inc.; **Steve Gragert** and the Will Rogers Commission; **Melissa Clark** and WPX; **David Kimmel** and SandRidge Energy; **Carolyn Sims** and Rose State College; **Kakio Richardson** and Metro Technology Centers; **Kenny Day** and Oklahoma Baptist University; **Colleen McCarty** and The Bama Companies; **Joy Hamilton** and **Jessica Ockershauser** and Chesapeake Energy; **Carla Brockman** and Devon Energy; **Gini Moore Campbell, Shelley Rowan** and **Tony A. Scott** with the Oklahoma Heritage Association; **Marsha Bold** and Hobby Lobby; **Daniel Yunker** and Kimray Inc.; **David Kimmel** SandRidge Energy; **Dr. Katherene Terrell** and the University of Central Oklahoma; **Jennifer Randell** and **Bree Dunham** with the Citizen Potawotami Nation Eagle Aviary.